Turnpike Gallery

John Newling

WEIGHT

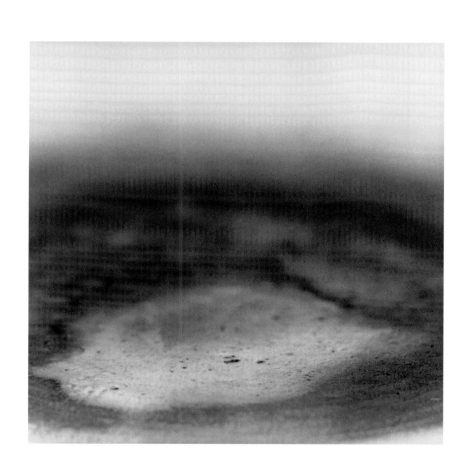

*The ten bowls containing the remains of the evaporation process
line the floor of the gallery/laboratory*

Objects on a laboratory bench include one of the individual 'cashier' books which hold all the measurements of weight taken during the process

During the seven days of experimentation, people outside the gallery were able to observe the process happening within via CCTV monitors placed along one side of the Turnpike Gallery

The Currency of Belief

Artranspennine98
at the Turnpike Gallery, Leigh
May 1998

Weight is an installation artwork by John Newling that defies easy or simple categorisation as the processes, objects, images and places it explores interweave in a myriad of interconnections and interrogations. **Weight** as artwork mutates towards empirical science demanding, for seven days, that the gallery become laboratory, where white-coated and supervised assistants, work methodological and highly structured procedures. Nor is the work confined to the physical space defined as gallery: by means of video surveillance the processes of the seven days of activity are broadcast to the outside and largely unknowing world. The gallery/laborarory processes spill out to a roof space where erected tents provide another atmosphere and serve as a sanctuary for the noxious fumes the alchemy of dirt removal requires.

After these seven days the gallery has become a ghost laboratory. Ten benches with the evidence of intense labour reveal a process of discovery. The discovery is both writ large on a wall in letters and numbers as well as being minutely documented through 'experiment data sheets' and again through ten small red cashier books. Each of the ten benches repeats the logic of the process where coins have been cleaned, their dirt measured and the result carefully documented and tabulated towards a final result. All experimental data passes through a central digital weighing machine, oozing out a large receipt, documenting the evidence of one thousand experiments on 50,000 coins apparently worth, on face value, £1000.

At each workstation, the handwriting, or the crossing out of figures, doodles in the cashier books attest to the human endeavour and personality of the now absent workers. The space has changed function from a place of intense activity to quieter observation, speculation and thought.

Ten large bowls, apparently sealed, bifurcate the gallery/laboratory space, containing the detritus from the systematic process of cleaning the coins. They are beautiful containers, clinical from the distance but more earthy and dirty as the eye inspects the contents. The contents are difficult to describe: they sort of resemble an evaporated, yet polluted, rock pool. The soft edges of dark shapes intensify to an oily mass.

THE FLOWS OF ECONOMY

In our daily transactions, we exchange a great deal. Words, coins, looks, feelings, beliefs and desires cross, mutate and realign in social, economic and artistic spheres. The value of these exchanges impinge on and inform both our conscious and unconscious worlds. **Weight** provides a formal experiment into some of these territories and forces questions around the discourses of economy, art and belief. Once we have decoded the experiment we are temporarily offered solace in the solution, the answer or the result. The answer is a magical number, a value, a significant clue. The answer is seven pence.

Money is the cornerstone of our economic lives. Coinage still features within our daily transactions and the principles of its usage are predicated on culturally accepted conventions of equivalence. Consumables, services, charities, property and certain pleasures can be bought, delivered or provided with money. An apple will, at a given time, in a given place be worth a certain monetary value. Yet every transaction demands a degree of faith – the coin or note must really be worth an equivalent value, otherwise economies would rapidly collapse. A two pence coin has no absolute value. Although apparently familiar, in shape, colour and feel, its currency is always subject to the wider economic picture.

Coins are both articles of faith and fortune (luck). We toss a coin, to determine an outcome of a game, a bet, a challenge. In our language they can also metaphorically allude to wealth (fortune). He has piles of money. But coinage is increasingly redundant, it is too heavy: it has weight. Coinage is too literal as money becomes virtual. Coins have lives outside their intended economic function, they serve our superstitions, fortunes and needs. Sometimes these functions are fused. When we hear a busker in the street playing a tune we like or know, do we toss a coin because we like the music or we wish to give some money so that the musician can eat?

The experience of **Weight** is arguably to collide with our culturally determined gaze. We do not know where we are as a laboratory, bank and gallery all provide different conventions of looking and behaving whereby processes are evaluated against expectation. We expect our counted coins to be worth a certain amount when we visit the bank. The emprical scientist seeks a result from an experiment with which to work a hypothesis. The gallery should yield some aesthetic or emotional experience. In **Weight** all of these expectations are questioned and questionable as the efficacy of these institutions fuses to form an over riding discourse on uncertainty. Simply put, we are not sure what we are witnessing.

CORPOREAL COIN: COINS CORPOREAL

John Newling's previous work has already revealed a little known relationship between the coin and the communion wafer. The two pence coin is stamped from sheets of mixed metal as are the wafers from sheets of flattened bread. They are the same size, the same shape and they pile similarly. This is no accident. Both coins and wafers stand in for something else, they occupy a place which is an absence, a place where literality and first order signification is culturally masked, subsumed to history or convention. Coins are money, where one thing stands for another and, within an economy at a given time, one thing is another.

At different times, two pence, a ruddy disc of metal, will have been an apple with its flesh, texture, shape and taste.

Wafers too work this metaphor: within the doctrine of transubstantiation, a consecration takes place in which the spiritual breaks into the material. This journey is one of the founding acts of faith where the bread (wafer) and the wine become, in substance, the body and blood of Christ. Once again, one thing is another. **Weight** extends the relationship of the literal and metaphorical by revealing, in the ten focal containers, human trace extracted from coins. Their materiality is only too apparent, magnified, documented and evidenced throughout the installation. In examining the carefully ordered and numbered jars of the post-experimental coins, on the ten work benches, there is no evidence they have changed by having their (or our) dirt removed. The coins are still dullish, used and mundane in their ordinariness. The seven pence of **Weight**, added through communion with social economies, and taken away by art and science, has not affected their appearance in any way. This may seem perplexing and provokes the thought, what would all the dirt in the world be worth if all coins were to be cleaned. No one knows the value of this secret economy or who owns or controls it, yet we all participate with our bodies, our pockets, our lives in these transactions. The logic of **Weight** dislodges expectations of value and appearance.

PLACING THE COUNT

From the 10th to the 17th May 1998 the Turnpike Gallery was the site of an experiment, and thereafter an installation remained within the gallery space until 16th August 1998. The seven days of experiment in May did not afford or allow for the casual 'gallery visitor' to see what was going on; the events could only be seen via the video relays of experimental data projected through the downstairs windows of the two storey municipal building. In some senses this process was a secret communion. This building houses a gallery on the top floor, and a library on the ground floor. It is a town centre context with Church and shopping centre framing the central site of the Turnpike. Although the building is relatively new in architecture and function, its name, Turnpike, alludes to toll gathering processes of the past. It was a tax collection point. Money is in its history and name. **Weight** revisits this past by *"recounting"(memory) the counting* in the sense of visiting a memory of past function, and making fresh the site, its place and the social context.

Weight tells us something about money at the end of the century: the human interactions with coins, both fleeting and profound, produce that hitherto secret economy of exchange. The ten bowls which are documents of this economy may yet become monuments, as coins, with their weight, become redundant to modes of exchange. They leave the tactile, human exchange of coins behind to monetary transfer through the virtual. Who can predict what traces a computer transfer of funds will produce. What belief systems, stories, rituals and languages will emerge can only be gauged over time. In the meantime, **Weight**, writes another story about money, this time around a gallery, but looking out at science with a solemn respect for the tangible and intangible nature of what things appear and what they really are.

Piers H Nicholls

Piers Nicholls was educated at the University of Leeds and at the University of Massachusetts. He has held posts as senior lecturer and course leader at Manchester Metropolitan University and Nottingham Trent University. He has written, broadcast and reviewed on critical theory, visual art, philosophy, performance and music. He is presently Dean of Art and Cultural Studies at Falmouth College of Arts.

The coins are stored in numbered containers which are cross referenced to the data sheets that hold the verification of the differing weights

Detail of a laboratory bench

The team of experiment assistants

An assistant at his bench records information into his individual cashier book from the data sheet

Consultations occur frequently during the latter stages of the process as the experiment gathers momentum

Work continues on the recording of data throughout the seven days

*On the roof space alongside the gallery/laboratory are the ten tents which serve as
fume chambers for the evaporation process*

Opposite:
Pouring the saturated solution into the evaporation dishes

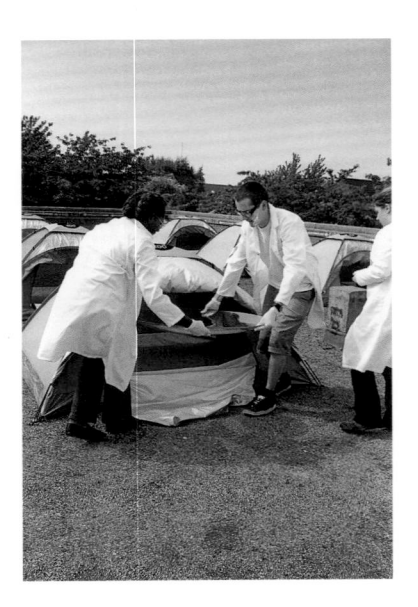 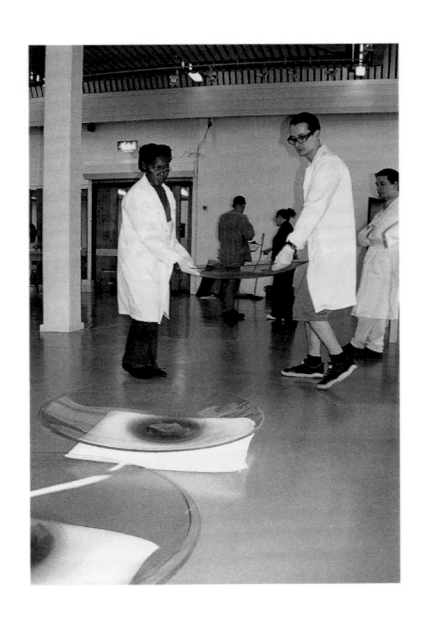

After one thousand experiments on 50,000 coins, the ten bowls containing the detritus left from the process are taken from the evaporation tents and placed in the gallery/laboratory

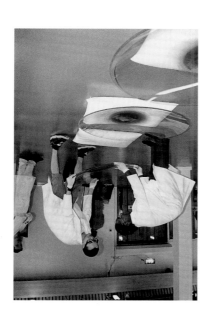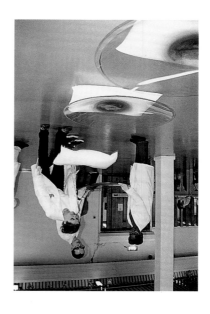

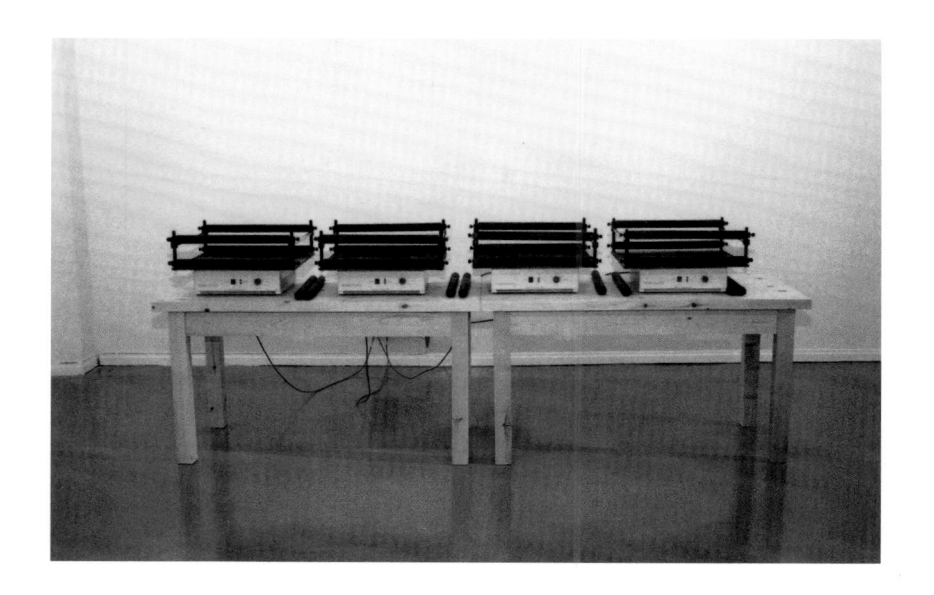

Opposite:
The central weighing machine prints out the receipt of all the experimental data

Above:
Working overnight, the agitation machines form part of the process of releasing
the dirt from the coins into the cyclohexane solution

During the experimentation period a microscope slide was taken from each batch of coins. The one thousand slides were then shown in the gallery/laboratory as part of the subsequent installation

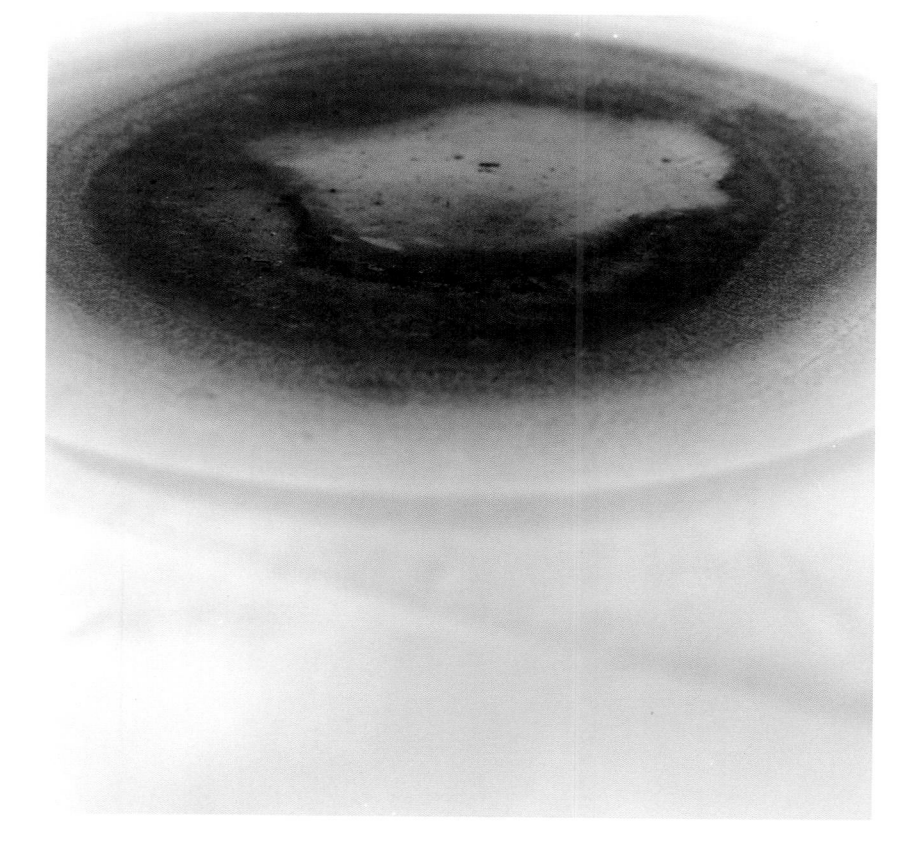

The soft edges of the distillate remaining in the glass intensifies to an oily mass at the centre

The final data sign. The result of the experiment is displayed on the wall of the gallery

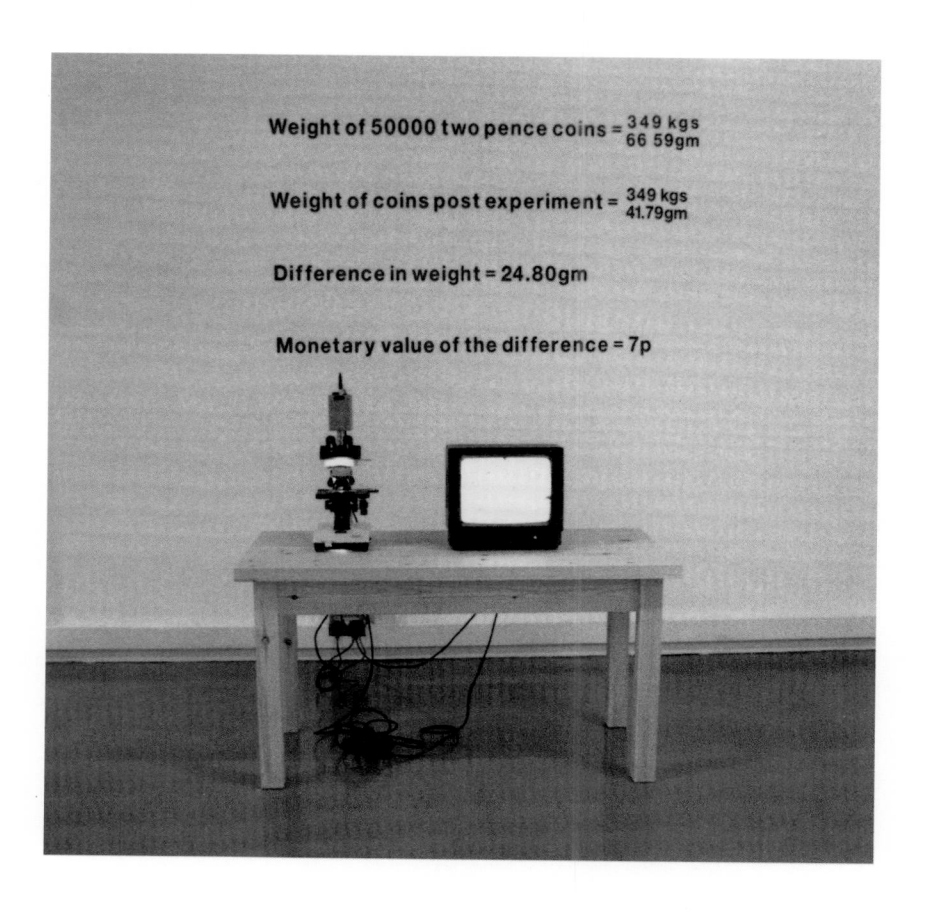

At the
close of the
experiment
the ten
focal
containers
of coin
residue are
placed
alongside
the
laboratory
benches.
The
laboratory
now
becomes
a gallery
and the
experiment
becomes
a public
installation

1. Glass containers, 250 ml x 1000.

2. Watch glass, 30 mm x 1000.

3. Microscope slides, x 1000.

4. Microscope cover slips, x 1000.

5. Microscope side box container, (100 slides to a box) x 10.

6. Glass funnel, 100 mm x 100.

7 Glass dropper, x 10.

8. Safety spectacles, x 10.

9. Respirator and filters, x 10.

10. Laboratory coats, x 10.

11. Balance A&D, multi-function.

12. Balance printer multi-function.

13. Microscope.

14. Colour camera, JVC.

15. JVC high colour monitor.

16. Shakers.

17. Cyclohexane.

The project has two distinct and related phases.

Phase 1. Phase 1 is the period of time, (seven to nine days) when the one thousand experiments are done by the ten project assistants.

Each assistant does one hundred experiments. Each assistant works at their designated work station. The ten work stations form the overall structure of the laboratory. As well as the work stations there will also be an electronic balance, an agitation machine, and a microscope connected to video outlet. At each work station there will be all the necessary instruments required to do the experiments.

The cyclohexane is stored within the parameters of the experiment site either in one volume or divided to the correspondent work stations.

As the coin residue material is formed each assistant will deposit the material into either one of ten glass dishes (one dish correspondent to each work station) or one large dish.

During this phase there will not be public access to the installation. However I would propose that during this period of activity a fixed camera will relay what is happening to a monitor that is positioned so the public will have a view of what is occurring.

The final aspect of this phase is the collation of the experimental data sheets to calculate:

The weight of the 50,000 coins prior to the experiments.
The weight of the coins post experiment.
The difference in weight.
The monetary equivalence of this difference.

Note: Between phase 1 (the experiments) and phase 2 (public access) the final data is installed within the parameters of the installation. Currently I envisage this sign to be written directly onto a selected wall site.

Phase 2. This is the public phase. Opening on the 23 May.

The public will see an installation that clearly is the site where experiments have occurred.

All evidence from phase 1 will remain on site. The absence of the phase 1 activity will give visual evidence as to what has occurred at the site. In this manner the ontology of what is left will reveal itself. During this phase of the installation, microscope slides from each of the one thousand experiments will be shown, at intervals, via the microscope onto the video monitor.

By way of further contextual information I would propose that copies of a commissioned essay, "The Currency of Belief" be available.

Schedule for the 1000 experiments

	Bench 1 = experiments 1–100	Bench 2 = experiments 101–200	
	Bench 3 = experiments 201–300	Bench 4 = experiments 301–400	
	Bench 5 = experiments 401–500	Bench 6 = experiments 501–600	
	Bench 7 = experiments 601–700	Bench 8 = experiments 701–800	
	Bench 9 = experiments 801–900	Bench 10 = experiments 901–1000	

Approximate schedule of the experiments   Number of completed experiments

Day: 1		Each bench worker prepares 20 of the jars. Priming the coins with the cyclohexane and starting the agitation process.	
Day: 2	The cyclohexane from the previous 20 jars is filtered into the large dish and the process of each experiment is carried out (see full experiment description for information.)	Each bench worker prepares 20 of the jars. Priming the coins with the cyclohexane and starting the agitation process.	200
Day: 3	The cyclohexane from the previous 20 jars is filtered into the large dish and the process of each experiment is carried out (see full experiment description for information.)	Each bench worker prepares 20 of the jars. Priming the coins with the cyclohexane and starting the agitation process.	400
Day: 4	The cyclohexane from the previous 20 jars is filtered into the large dish and the process of each experiment is carried out (see full experiment description for information.)	Each bench worker prepares 20 of the jars. Priming the coins with the cyclohexane and starting the agitation process.	600
Day: 5	The cyclohexane from the previous 20 jars is filtered into the large dish and the process of each experiment is carried out (see full experiment description for information.)	Each bench worker prepares 20 of the jars. Priming the coins with the cyclohexane and starting the agitation process.	800
Day: 6	The cyclohexane from the previous 20 jars is filtered into the large dish and the process of each experiment is carried out (see full experiment description for information.)		1000
Day: 7	Final calculation of the discrepancy between the weight of the coins before the experiment and after. Calculation of hypothetical value of the coin residue.		

Published by Turnpike Gallery

WEIGHT

at the Turnpike Gallery

May 1998

Civic Square

Leigh

WN7 1EB

Telephone: 01942 404 469

Facsimile: 01942 404 447

Acknowledgements

The Turnpike Gallery would like to thank John Newling
for his commitment and enthusiasm throughout
this project, Piers H Nicholls for his insightful essay,
Mark Shelton of Scientific Laboratory Supplies Ltd,
The Nottingham Trent University, Paul Bayley,
Robert Hopper from artranspennine98 and to the Lab
Assistants for their help: Ansie Frost, Richard Hughes,
Andrew Martin, Cathy Masthias, Islamiat Onigbanjo,
Kevin Pemberton, Barry Renshaw, Leanne Riley,
Otto Smart and Angela Wildman.

Andrea Hawkins

Gallery Officer

ISBN 0 952947 02 1

Design: A W @ Axis, Manchester

alan@axis.zen.co.uk

Photography: Paula Latham

Print and repro: Pale Green Press, London

Weight of 20000 two pence coins = 66.59 gm
349 kgs

Weight of coins boat experiment = 41.79 gm
349 kgs

Difference in weight = 24.80 gm

Monetary value of the difference = 5p